D1541397

PICTURE A COUNTRY

Spain

Henry Pluckrose

W
FRANKLIN WATTS
A Division of Grolier Publishing
NEW YORK • LONDON • HONG KONG • SYDNEY
DANBURY, CONNECTICUT

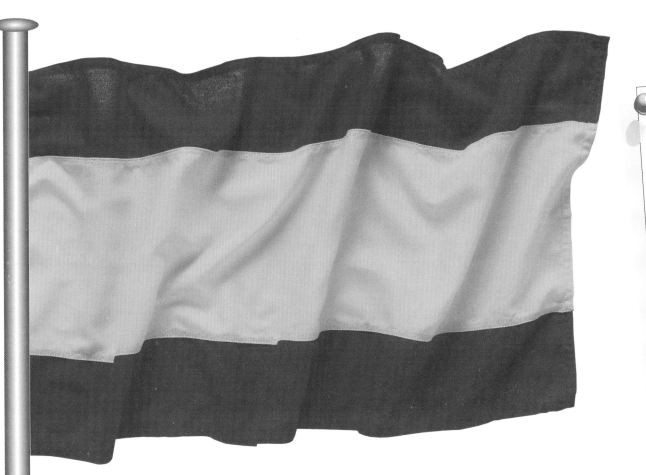

This is the Spanish flag.

First published by Franklin Watts in 1998
First American edition 1998 by
Franklin Watts
A Division of Grolier Publishing
90 Sherman Turnpike
Danbury, CT 06816
Visit Franklin Watts on the Internet at:
http://publishing.grolier.com

Library of Congress Cataloging-in-Publication Data
Pluckrose, Henry Arthur.
    Spain / Henry Pluckrose.
        p. cm. -- (Picture a country)
    Includes index.
    Summary: A simple introduction to the geography, people,
culture, and interesting sites of Spain.
    ISBN 0-531-11510-0 (lib. bdg.)   0-531-15377-0 (pbk.)
    1. Spain--Juvenile literature. [1. Spain.] I. Title.
II. Series: Pluckrose, Henry Arthur. Picture a country.
DT17.P58 1998   98-5497
946--DC21   CIP
                                                       AC

Series editor: Rachel Cooke
Series designer: Kirstie Billingham
Picture research: Juliet Duff
Printed in Great Britain

Photographic acknowledgments:

Cover: J. Allan Cash t, Medimage br (Anthony King),
Telegraph Colour Library bl (G. Van der Elst).

AKG, London p. 25;
J. Allan Cash pp. 8, 15, 29;
Anthony Blake Photo Library p. 22b (G. Buntrock);
Getty Images pp. 10 (Robert Frerck), 13t (David Hanson),
18 (Oliver Benn), 23 (Nadia Mackenzie), 28b (Sylvain
Grandadam);
Robert Harding Picture Library p. 21;
The Hutchison Library p. 19;
Images Colour Library pp. 13b, 28t;
Images Select p. 22t (Chris Fairclough);
Link p. 20 (Orde Eliason);
Medimage pp. 9, 17, 16 (Anthony King);
Spectrum Colour Library pp. 11, 16, 27;
Telegraph Colour Library pp. 12, 14 (G. Van der Elst), 24.

All other photography by Steve Shott.
Map by Julian Baker.

Contents

Where Is Spain?

This is a map of Spain.
Spain is the third largest country in Europe. The Balearic Islands in the Mediterranean Sea and the Canary Islands in the Atlantic Ocean are also part of Spain.

Here are some Spanish stamps and money.

Spanish money is counted in pesetas.

FRANCE

BAY OF BISCAY

SPAIN

Altamira Bilbao

Vitoria Pyrenees Mountains

Ebro River

Douro River Zaragoza

CATALONIA COSTA BRAVA

Segovia

Tarragona Barcelona

PORTUGAL

Madrid

Tagus River

Toledo

BALEARIC ISLANDS

Valencia

Guadiana River

Guadalquivir River Córdoba

ANDALUSIA

MEDITERRANEAN SEA

Casares

ATLANTIC OCEAN

ALGERIA

MOROCCO

The Spanish Landscape

Spain is a country of great plains, hills, and high mountains.
Five important rivers run through Spain — the Douro, Ebro, Guadiana, Guadalquivir, and Tagus.

The Pyrenees Mountains divide Spain from France.

This bridge over the Guadiana River marks the border between Spain and Portugal. The Spanish word for "river" is "rio".

Spanish summers are hot and dry, but sometimes there are sudden storms. The winters are cold and wet in northern and central Spain. In the south, they are mild.

The Spanish People

People first lived in Spain more than 800,000 years ago.
We know about the people who once lived in Spain by the things they left behind.

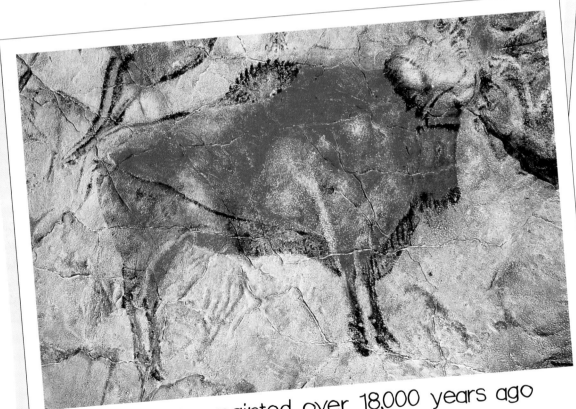

This bison was painted over 18,000 years ago on a cave wall in Altamira.

This aqueduct in Segovia was built by the Romans when they ruled Spain. An aqueduct carries water.

Today, nearly 40 million people live in Spain.

Where They Live

Most Spanish people live in villages and small towns.

This is the small town of Casares in southern Spain.

There are some cities —
Madrid, Barcelona, Bilbao,
Valencia, Vitoria, and Zaragoza.

Barcelona is the capital of the Catalonia region, where most people speak Catalan rather than Spanish.

A statue of Christopher Columbus stands in Barcelona. He sailed from Spain to discover America.

The Capital City

This is the Plaza de la Cibeles, a great square at the center of Madrid.

There is a market every Sunday in Madrid called El Rastro. People sell second-hand goods and antiques.

Madrid is the capital of Spain.
More than three million people live there.
Madrid is a city of fine buildings,
museums, and parks.

At Work

Spanish workers build ships and cars and make some of the electrical goods we use in our homes.

This factory in Tarragona processes oil and makes different things from it, including plastics and gasoline.

These fishermen are repairing their nets before their next trip out to sea.

Around the coast of Spain, there are many fishing villages. The fishermen travel thousands of miles across the sea to catch cod, sardines, and tuna.

Olive trees are planted in lines, which stretch for hundreds of miles across the Spanish countryside.

Farming

Spanish farmers are famous for their olives and almonds.

These Spanish farmworkers are packing celery.
The celery will be sold in stores all over Europe.

Farmers also grow barley, wheat, corn, and rice; oranges, lemons, peaches and grapes; and potatoes, onions, and other vegetables. They often raise sheep and cows.

Family Life

Spanish families do a lot together.
Often grandparents, parents, and
children live in the same house.

This mother and her son are looking at sneakers
in a market in Zaragoza.

Meals are important times for the family
to get together.
They eat at lunchtime and late in the evening.
In the afternoon, most people have a rest.
This rest is called a siesta.

Spanish Food

People in different parts of Spain enjoy different kinds of food.

Cured meats and sausages are eaten all over Spain.

Eastern Spain is known for paella – rice served with fish, meat, peppers, and beans.

Shopkeepers make beautiful displays with the high-quality Spanish fruit and vegetables.

In northern Spain, meals include sardines, lobster, tuna, pork, and lamb.

In southern Spain, people enjoy cold soups, barbecued meats, squid, olives, figs, melons, and oranges.

Out and About

Spaniards enjoy tennis, cycling, golf, skiing and all kinds of water sports. Bullfighting is a popular Spanish sport, though many people think it is cruel.

White-water rafting has become a popular sport on the fast-moving mountain rivers of the Pyrenees.

This painting of a Spanish family is by
Bartolomé Murillo (1617-1682).

People in Spain often visit museums
and art galleries.
They can see works by famous Spanish artists—
Velázquez, Murillo, Goya, and Picasso.

Fiestas and Dancing

In the week before Easter in the city of Córdoba, there are processions through the streets.
This is the Palm Sunday procession.

Most Spanish people are Roman Catholics.
Important saints' days are celebrated
with fiestas (festivals).
Dancing and music are part of every fiesta.

The flamenco is a gypsy dance from Andalusia.
The dancers are accompanied by guitars and
wooden castanets.

Many tourists visit the ancient city of Toledo.

The Sagrada Familia church in Barcelona, designed by Antonio Gaudi (1852-1926), is still being built.

Visiting Spain

Each year more than 20 million tourists go to Spain on vacation.
They visit Spain to see its beautiful cities, churches, palaces, and castles or to walk in its mountains.
But most tourists go to relax on its sunny beaches.

This is a beach on Spain's Costa Brava.

Index

About This Book

The last decade of the 20th century has been marked by an explosion in communications technology. The effect of this revolution upon the young child should not be underestimated. The television set brings a cascade of ever-changing images from around the world into the home, but the information presented is only on the screen for a few moments before the program moves on to consider some other issue.

Instant pictures, instant information do not easily satisfy young children's emotional and intellectual needs. Young children take time to assimilate knowledge, to relate what they already know to ideas and information that are new.

The books in this series seek to provide snapshots of everyday life in countries in different parts of the world. The images have been selected to encourage the young reader to look, to question, to talk. Unlike the TV picture, each page can be studied for as long as is necessary and subsequently returned to as a point of reference. For example, a Spanish shop or market might be compared with one in their own area; a discussion might develop about the ways in which food is prepared and eaten in a country whose culture and customs are different from their own.

The comparison of similarity and difference is the recurring theme in each of the titles in this series. People in different lands are superficially different. Where they live (the climate and terrain) obviously shapes the sort of houses that are built, but people across the world need shelter; coins may look different, but in each country people use money.

At a time when the world seems to be shrinking, it is important for children to be given the opportunity to focus upon those things that are common to all the peoples of the world. By exploring the themes touched upon in the book, children will begin to appreciate that there are strands in the everyday life of human beings that are universal.